OUT OF THE SLIPPERY PIT

Linda Palucci

chipmunkapublishing
the mental health publisher
empowering people with cancer

Linda Palucci

All rights reserved, no part of this publication may be reproduced by any means, electronic, mechanical photocopying, documentary, film or in any other format without prior written permission of the publisher.

> Published by
> Chipmunkapublishing
> PO Box 6872
> Brentwood
> Essex CM13 1ZT
> United Kingdom

http://www.chipmunkapublishing.com

Copyright © Linda Palucci 2008

Chipmunkapublishing gratefully acknowledges the support of Arts Council England.

Linda Palucci

OUT OF THE SLIPPERY PIT

The first time was rough. I sat there wondering what am I doing here? The men were not appealing, and the music was too loud. I felt dead inside. Three gals I met at THEOS - a group for widow/widowers - and I, have been going to a couple of single dances, lately.

Rosemary, the proprietor, asked why I was not dancing. I burst out, "I can't feel the music!" This was true, the music was gone. Nothing seemed important. I was so tight. "THEY" say "IT" gets better in time, if one works at "IT". In the beginning a widow can sit at home and cry. After a while, "THEY" say she must get back into the world. Pick up the pieces, and make a new life.
Like the Phoenix, from the ashes of before.

I sat there with tears I could not restrain, running down my cheeks. It has been almost one year. When do you begin to feel like a person again? I am trying.
"THEOS" stands for They Help Each Other Spiritually. To join you must be a widow or widower. It is helpful for new members to associate with those who have survived widowhood for various lengths of time. I believe only someone who has experienced the death of a spouse can really understand the pain and confusion.
Maybe only children, as I am, can adjust simply because we start out alone. We had only

ourselves to depend on when we were young. I don't know if this is true or not, just a personal theory. Or, it makes us feel more alone.

I remember clearly when the horror started. I had gone to work. Our daughter Cheryl had taken Gene to the Doctor. He had been experiencing headaches and double-vision for a few weeks and went to check it out. The doctor had suggested an eye exam. He'd also had him get an MRI. I had never heard of an MRI, that I could remember. Now, today he would see what our Doctor had found.
He recommended a Neuro-surgeon.
Gene called me at the office. "It don't look good for The Kid," he said, referring to himself, as "The Kid".
"What do you mean?" I whispered, my heart suddenly racing. I knew in my head what he meant, but my heart did not want to hear it. That was it. That simple sentence, the beginning of hell.

In the beginning the Nero-surgeon said, "It's not life-threatening." At first they were not certain if it was a stroke or tumor.

June 10th, 1991. I lost my husband. My wonderful, adorable mate. He had been diagnosed with an in-operable brain tumor. Our doctor, on the phone, attempted to explain it to me, "It's a tragedy!"
"No!" My heart screamed. "He'll be OK. This can't be happening."
He had his beautiful dark brown wavy hair shaved

to make it easier for the radiation treatment. They had to draw lines on his head. His last trip to his barber.

He started to lose his balance. One night he went upstairs to undress for bed. He fell against the dresser and gashed his left ear. I had fallen asleep on the couch downstairs, and did not hear him. Fortunately, Chris and Greg, two of our sons were upstairs; they heard him fall and took him to the hospital. They stitched his ear together.

By September, he could not sleep lying down. He sat all night in his recliner. The doctor checked him. He had pneumonia. He was in the hospital a week, with a tube under his arm into his lung. When he came home we decided he should not smoke. Then he began to sneak them from us. Soon he was back to smoking. Because he was just sitting, and nervous; he began to smoke more and more.
Strangely, the cigarettes were not an issue as far as the doctors were concerned.
Somewhere around this time, at the Doctor's office for a consultation, I remember Gene asked, "Are you still saying this is not life threatening?" I recall feeling dread, when the doctor did not answer.

He fell against a window in the dining room, broke a pane, and a glass table, holding plants. We moved our bed downstairs to the den, after he stumbled on the last three steps coming down one morning. I caught him in my arms.

Linda Palucci

What told me to go to the bottom of the stairs? I had been getting ready for work. Doing my hair in the downstairs bathroom. I was vaguely aware he was coming down, and for some unknown reason I rushed to the steps, just in time to catch him. I don't know how I was able to stop his fall, the front door was open, he was headed for the doorknob and window.

Something changed between us; I was no longer his wife. I became his caretaker. I was still busy in this world, but he was preparing for the next. It's hard to explain. He was involved with himself. It was a subtle change. He kind of withdrew from us. Maybe it was in self defense.

After the bed was moved one of us helped him up and down the stairs to bathe. Peter, our son-in-law, installed a bar in the tub. Someone had to be with him because he really was very unsteady when he got up.

He had radiation. Our daughter, Cheryl, came over daily and drove him to the hospital. I was still working. She stayed with him until I got home.

There was a physical therapist coming to the house a couple of times a week. He accomplished, little, other than giving Gene more pain. His strength was deteriorating. His legs could not support him; he started to use a cane. His beautiful brown eyes with those long lashes could no longer read the newspaper.

He saw double with both eyes open. To see normal, he kept one eye shut. He tried a patch, our granddaughter, Heather, said it made him look like a pirate.
Near the end of November he began therapy at the hospital. He was bouncing a ball with his left hand, his weak side. He was supposed to be holding on to a bar with his right hand. The ball bounced away, he let go of the bar to retrieve it and fell on his face. Down to the emergency room. They said he was OK.

He did have an egg on his forehead. The doctors were prescribing physical therapy. They wouldn't do that if he was going to die. I rationalized. This encouraged my fantasy that every thing would be all right. He was too young to die, at only 55.

From June to the beginning of December I tried to pretend, unable to accept what was really happening. Gene was dying. Our family was losing father, husband, and brother. His sisters, Audrey and Geri, came over at least once a week. We live about thirty miles from them. They were so much help. They always tried to bring him a special treat.

I heard from the doctor, December 3rd. The treatment had not helped. I was in my office. I was so shocked I could not talk. I said goodbye to the doctor, hung up and called Cheryl at home. She asked what the doctor had said. All I could manage was, "it doesn't look good." She phoned the doctor for more information.

She called me back. "The doctor said, in a few months he'll get worse, he'll probably slip into a coma." I broke down at my desk, put my head down, and finally cried great heart-wrenching sobs.

A co-worker came in, closed my door handed me a hand full of tissue. I remember she said, "we've wondered, how you've gotten this far."
I had tried to pretend everything was fine, while I was at work. It was the only thing keeping me half-way sane. In January, the business went the way of many recently, it closed, and I was laid off. It was the 16th - our 32nd wedding anniversary. Looking back at those months now, I realise I reacted like an ostrich. I wish I could have talked to him more about what was happening. I remember one time we were sitting at the table. He said, "I'll probably die before you."
I turned off that conversation for many months. I could not remember what he had said next. Long after, it came to me. He had finished with, "Don't think you are alone you have my sisters and our family." I did not want to hear it. I could not accept it.

After Gene died, I went to the library. Looked up 'grief' in the card catalog. Reading helped me understand my reactions were normal. I was in the denial stage. I don't think I really accepted he was going to die. It was just inconceivable. It could not be happening.

I was so afraid he would get worse and worse until he was not even himself. Some people go on for years like vegetables. My constant prayer was, "please God, take him or heal him."

Linda Palucci

Chapter 2

From here on, the bold print is exactly what I wrote at the time. I found it helped to write my thoughts. I'm glad I did.

My husband is 'gone', in his place; a shadow of him sits in his chair, sleeps in our bed and knows all of us. This feeling of sitting around a 'death bed' is on the entire family. We feel as if our lives are on hold. His strength is gone both mentally and physically. We can no longer discuss our problems with him. He does not need stress. We have divided his stress among us. Childlike, he has gone 'into himself' where only his needs are relevant. We all eat Advil like M&M's, cry out of his sight and move around in a daze. I might as well put Advil in a candy dish.

If I yell at him, he becomes hurt and I feel horrible guilt.
He who used to yell about everything now can barely be heard or understood. This 'demon thing' in his head is slowly robbing us of the leader of the family. And, while we all try to make believe he still has the position, we are the ones who worry, work and watch.

Nothing seems important; no one makes plans too far ahead. I have a glimmer of

Linda Palucci

hope way down deep, (or is it wishful thinking?) that he will come back to his old self. Meanwhile I think of what funeral parlor and cemetery I may have to contact soon.

I prayed. Our friends prayed; friends and family had others praying. I became confused in my faith. I felt sure a miracle would happen. I felt anger, not so much at God, but at life. Why were we born, why did we love if only to lose? How does the world function at all? Practically everyone has had a disaster of some sort. Death visits everyone indiscriminately. If everyone who has lost a loved one is as muddled as I am, how does anything get done at all?
I later discovered this confusion is also typical. I was experiencing preliminary grief. I remember very little regarding that time. If I had not kept a journal I would not have any idea of what happened. Most this is copied exactly as I wrote at the time.
We had not told Gene the doctor said the radiation had not worked. I told him it had helped and his muscles were weak from sitting. By telling him the Doctors offered little hope, would have made it real.
Our son, Russ, told me his mother-in-law, Helen, had read about a hospital on Staten Island, which used laser to eliminate tumors.

Russ contacted Staten Island University Hospital. We sent MRI's

over to them. What a hassle, but it feels good to be doing something
instead of just sitting. We may be chasing rainbows but we have to try.

Always, the situation follows all of us, even though we try to act natural.
People ask, 'how are you doing?'
I answer, 'hanging in there.' How can I scream at them, 'my world is falling apart?' I know they ask because they are concerned.

Neither Gene nor I were very patient. We are both impulsive. We knew each other 3 months and got married. It is hard for us to wait. Is the impetuous young man still there? The one who said, 'let's get your diamonds now. If you don't get them now, you never will.' So we got them, and for 32 years they have twinkled on my left hand.

He staggers, he falls, he keeps asking for cigarettes - one after the other - is he trying to hurry it up?

When he used to talk to us he would glaze in mirrors or reflective surfaces, because he was good looking. Now his head is bald from radiation. Did it help, or only prolong the agony? He keeps one eye open and the other shut to see single. His mouth droops to the left. He only looks in the mirror when he shaves.

Linda Palucci

Now he sits in his chair under a blanket and watches TV. His 20/20 vision is double, reading is almost impossible.

He was always outgoing, he did boy scouts, was a volunteer fireman, managed little league. He loved kids and made a great manager. He had a boy on his team with one hand. He helped and encouraged him. One day the boy hit a home run. I'll never forget. The parents and players on both sides cheered him as he ran the bases. It was one of those rare moments when we are all part of God's children.

My stomach knots, a tight feeling in the pit. How long? How much can our family stand? Why? Oh God, my prayer is what Jesus said to Judas, 'What you must do, do quickly.' But maybe God has other plans. Please, God, whatever thy will.

Sometimes, as I help him to the bed or bathroom, he cuddles me or holds me tight like he used to. It feels so good. I remember how he always signed his cards to me. 'Love always, Gene.' God, it hurts so much. Tears are always ready to flow. I hardly ever wear mascara any more, because it is usually all over my face. How can this be happening? My other half is dying before my eyes. My nerves are so tight my throat is stiff and closed. I feel like I have a permanent fur ball in there.

My friend, Angela, advised me to contact

Linda Palucci

Hospice. She said they really helped when her father died. But if I do - that will mean I admit he is dying. Maybe I am not ready for that. Right now, I thank God each morning I wake up next to him cuddled around me.

I'm so confused. I'm so tired. I love Angie, we've known each other since sixth grade. Her advice is probably good. But I remember what my Aunt said when my Uncle died. 'I've lost my best friend.'

It is one thing with a parent and another with your mate.

He watches TV, like it is real. He will say something like, 'look at that old car, it's a Merc.' I think, 'who cares?'

Who cares? 'Things' are just 'things'. All we possess, all these 'things' cluttering up the house, what use are they? All so unimportant, so meaningless. We drag all this 'stuff' though our lives. At the end we leave it.
I help him walk, his arm around my shoulder, my arm around him tight as he staggers. I think of how he ran from right field to left to catch a fly on the run. He was good.

Now he scratches his bald head which is slowly growing in. He constantly asks if the doors are locked. I realise it is because he feels so vulnerable.
I can't get enthused over anything. I think my mind

Linda Palucci

blocks feelings because it hurts so much to feel. There are five stages of grief, denial, anger, bargaining, depression, and acceptance. I experience all five at times. I don't feel as if I have a life. I am neither wife nor widow. It's as though I have been deserted, and feel anger at him for doing this to me, to us, to our family. I understand it is not his fault and feel guilt at emotions I can not control.

Keeping the information of how serious his condition is, is tearing me apart. We have always been honest with each other. I don't feel as if we are a team anymore.

God, I'm hurting so bad. The future looks bleak and the present is absolute hell.
Russ, Cheryl, Gene and I went to Staten Island University Hospital toward the end of January.

All the way down and back it was, 'give me a cigarette.' Over and over and over. Until we were all ready to toss him and the cigarettes out of the car.

When we arrived - a few minutes late, but not too bad considering the drive was difficult - we didn't know where we were going, plus it rained hard and was very foggy. We went to several buildings before we found the correct one.
 'I told you on the phone it was building number one,' said the nurse at the desk.
 "We were lucky we found Staten Island," said

Linda Palucci

Russ.

For the first time I felt a glimmer of real hope. The process is called Stereotactic Radiosurgery. Many thin beams are directed at the tumor. They get it in a cross-fire. The process itself is short, but the preparation takes most of the day. They told us the success rate is 95%.

When the Doctor entered Cheryl said, 'We were told it was in-operable.'
He said 'Almost in-operable. Gene was in his wheelchair telling the three doctors present, the tumor was gone. But the doctors were looking at the MRI's. I admitted then to Gene, we had not told him everything. Then I told him we had been looking for alternatives.

Even to this day, I'm not sure if I did right. But he was always so much a mind over matter person. I was afraid if he knew how bad he really was, he would give up completely.

We decided to give the treatment a chance. It seemed to be the only way.

Linda Palucci

Chapter 3

The treatment was scheduled for February 3rd. He would be admitted Sunday, February 2nd.

My friend Janet came for a few days before Gene was to go. I'm glad, because it kept me occupied. She had made a quilt for Gene.

A couple of months ago she had broken her hip and was on crutches. She stayed until Thursday and helped us all make it though the week.

This morning S.LU.H. is scheduled to call and tell us what time to be there. My heart is beating fast - we are embarking on a journey of life or death. The next few days will affect our entire future.

If they succeed in eliminating the tumour it is still a long road back. His muscles are so weak from eight months of sitting, he can barely walk. It will be a long time before he gets his strength back. I feel numb.

His sister, Geri, her husband, Eddie, and our niece, Stacy, were here last night. More bad news - Eddie has to have a tumour removed from where he had his kidney removed. Poor Geri, her brother and husband both to have operations.
There is some good news, our son Scott and

Linda Palucci

his wife Debbie are going to have a baby.

Now it's 7:30 Sunday morning, Feb 2, 1992 and I'm a total basket case. I'm sitting in the kitchen waiting for coffee to finish. Cat and dog have been out and in, and are under the table eating their breakfast. Now the wait for the call from the hospital.

Last night was terrible. Gene and I went to bed around eleven. Around two, he called to Greg, who was in the living-room to come get him. He wanted to watch TV.

Poor Greg is a bundle of nerves. I did not realise how stressed he is too. He screamed and yelled at Gene just like I do when I get absolutely strung out. It's so frustrating when Gene will not co-operate. Greg was tired and did not want Gene up again.

He knew he would sit and smoke and had to be watched. Because his hands are unsteady, he keeps dropping cigarettes. There are little burns all over the place. He got Gene to his chair and yelled for me to get up. Of course, I was already awake, after all the racket those two made. Greg does not feel good, and I know he's upset. Yesterday all he did was eat all day long.

There are people who yell about everything, Gene was one and so was Cheryl, and Scott, also a few of our relatives. Chris, Russ, Greg and I usually do not. We are patient.

We felt so defenceless - we yelled at Gene because we had lost all control over the situation. Another grief symptom. We were so angry. I did not understand then. We were feeling powerless and yelled at everything and everybody. Gene asked for a cigarette and sometimes I threw them at him and shrieked, "You'll survive the tumour and kill yourself from cigarettes." Then I felt terrible remorse for being cruel.

One time he said sadly, "You're not my Linda anymore."

"How can I be? I'm scared senseless," I screeched

I came out and lay on the sofa with my pillow and slept off and on. Finally, I got Gene back to bed. Later Greg came down to check on him, he was relieved Gene was in bed. I was too restless to go to bed so I watched Nick at night till around 4:00.

It is 9:20; I'm wandering around doing odds and ends things. The cordless phone is in my pocket. The cat and dog trail me everywhere. I'm a nervous wreck. It's cold and very windy today, but at least the sun is shinning. Gene's tossing around in there.

I'm basically packed, just last minute

things to throw in. I wish I knew what I'm doing.

Well, Gene is up, now. I dragged him into the bathroom, cat and dog following. My stomach is one big knot. I chased the critters out, gave him his cigarette. Now the wait till he's done, drag him to his chair, give him coffee and something to eat. I guess we wait.

Now it is 9:35. I want to get this show on the road. I'm smoking one after the other. He probably will too. I want to go up and shower and dress. Maybe Chris or Greg will get up. Maybe I'll cook some bacon.

9:45 the hospital just called. Bed is ready.

Linda Palucci

Chapter 4

We left home six minutes to noon. February 2nd. We arrived at hospital around 1:30. The traffic was moderate, thank God. We got Gene settled in his room. Number 16.
I took a room at the Holiday Inn on Richmond Ave. Very nice.

There were closer motels, but the nurses warned me about them.
I also toured most of Staten Island, until I bought a map and asked directions.
Now it is Monday. I could not fall asleep when I got back to my room, until around midnight.

Woke up at 5:00. Motel does not serve coffee till 7:00. Finally, I went down for coffee and English muffin. Brought some coffee back to my room. I'm just sitting here looking out the window, thinking what am I doing here? I have to get over to the hospital. At last, after five cups I feel almost alive. The waitress's mother is also at S.LU.H.- we talked for a while. Staten Island is really pretty.

I am so nervous. I want to be there (at hospital) and yet all I do is sit and think.

I got to the hospital at 9:30. They were just taking him down for a CAT scan. He had been given Valium so he was very groggy. He had a metal ring around his head with screws connecting it to him. He looked so pathetic, but everyone seemed to say things were going well. Thank God. I'm sitting in the waiting room now because his room is being cleaned.

He's back in his room and we are watching 'Price is Right' on a six inch television. Doctors were in, and said the CAT scan looked good. They'll be doing procedure later around three-thirty. Nurse just came to change his IV. Lunch came.
Now the afternoon wait until he goes down. I went out to K-mart. He was napping and I was restless. I found some little things to bring home for Heather and Shannon.
Now it's almost three o'clock. The Doctors said they would do it at three-thirty. God guide them.

Everything seems so casual - not like it's the important thing that it is. He's just laying quiet watching Hawaii 5 0. I feel like screaming.

Well, around four-thirty this nice big orderly named Anthony came up, and down we went. The setup there was awesome. Looked like the deck of the USS Enterprise. Computers everywhere. The machine itself was unbelievable. We went into a pink brick room, where they put him on a table and bombarded him with rays. It took almost half an hour. They removed his head band and rolled him out.

They said it went very well. He still has to stay for a couple of days for observation. When we got upstairs dinner was served and he ate very well. I don't know if it's my imagination but he looks better already. While he was in the treatment. I read psalms. It was very comforting.

He's watching TV now. He said, 'if this doesn't work, forget it.'
Well, it's Tuesday morning February 4th. I feel fairly relaxed compared to how I have felt for the last few months. My main complaint is not much to watch on TV. I don't know how anyone can sit around doing nothing, so boring.

All the kids called me here to see how Gene made out. Janet and Tony called Gene. Tony said He sounded better.

We are home now feels good, Thursday evening, Gene read the paper for the first time in ages. He was also looking at photos. Seems much more alert. Using his eyes more. His hands are steady. His mouth is not drooping. But he is very tired. (me too)

The Doctors told us it would be a few weeks until the tumor has shrunk down.
There may be a slight set back. They'll call us in about 6 weeks to check on how he is doing, and set up an appointment.
Everyone called or came to see how he's doing. It looks so good to see him sitting straighter. We went to bed around 10:00. Best sleep in a long time.

Linda Palucci

He's sleeping good. It's 8:15 Friday morning. I noticed he kicked the cover off him a couple of times. Maybe he's not as cold as he was, maybe he won't be able to sleep in sweat suits like he's been doing. His legs are very weak. Last night when I was helping him to the bath room he kept collapsing. I had to scream for Chris, he was up in his room. Good thing he heard me. We have to build up his muscles again. I had better study physical therapy.
So much is running though my head. My mind can not rest. So much to think about. Gene, money, mortgage, millions of details.

Linda Palucci

Chapter 5

GMAC called, they want money by mid-week. God help me with these stupid money problems. Just enough to get my bills paid. So I don't get nagged. Just enough to afford what we have. So many things have had to be done. Furnace, roof, truck tire, cat, dishwasher, money for Holiday Inn. Money has to go places I really don't have it for right now. God I wish I didn't have to worry about money too.

It's 3:30 AM Saturday February 8th. Donna, Russ's wife is sick and our granddaughter Shannon is here. Shannon fell asleep on the couch watching Cinderella. She woke up and wanted her pj's on. So I got her ready and had just gone upstairs with her to put her in bed.

Suddenly I heard a THUMP down stairs. I ran down and Gene was on the living room floor. He looked like a praying Hindu. Greg also heard the noise and ran down. He took him to the bathroom and we got him back to bed. He had a rug burn on his forehead. Greg told him he was making it hard for him to give people good reports.

I was upstairs a matter of seconds. I don't know why he got up.
Now Shannon is sleeping upstairs. Gene is sleeping and I'm wide awake. I'm amazed he made it as far as the living room. Guess I'll read for awhile. Gene woke up around 9:00. I helped

him to the bathroom. I noticed he walked taller, he was not bent over he walked better also.

It's Sunday morning. Gene just asked me where Cheryl was, I said she was home. He said, 'I don't see her.'
I said she's at her house. He looked blank, when I said she was at her house. He swore and said 'Don't play around with me.'
When he woke up this morning he was calling for his sister Audrey. This is a bit unsettling.

It's 6:00 AM Monday. I got broken up sleep, but at least I got some sleep. Boy is it cold outside. Shannon slept in bed upstairs and later in my chair.
Somehow Gene fell? out of bed. He was sitting on the floor at the foot of the bed. I managed to get him back up again. Guess he'll go back to sleep. Last night he asked Greg if his firehouse jacket was in the closet. Greg showed it to him. Gene mumbled something about fruit in the pocket.
When I put him in bed yesterday he asked where his TV was. (It was in the living room, he should know that.)

He's really doing a lot of sleeping right now. The cat's in a wild mood, dog too. I let them both out. Don't think they'll stay out long, real cold out there. Cheryl is sick she called yesterday. Donna is sick. Greg doesn't feel too good. I hate February.
It's 2:40 PM Monday. Gene was up, very quiet,

went back to sleep. Cheryl, bless her heart came over and took Shannon and Heather for a ride. Nice and quiet here now. Gene's still nagging for cigarettes.

Its 10:30 Tues AM. Shannon is here. Cheryl has no heat. Peter is working. I just got a turkey in the oven. Gene is sleeping. He sleeps a lot wonder if that is normal. I feel like a wandering soul. I don't know what we are going to do. His insurance benefits ended the 9th. I need Cheryl. I can't think anymore.

During this time Cheryl was doing all the paper work. So much was involved. She applied for Social Security. It had just started in December. He had to be out of work for six months. There were tons of forms for the insurance, plus trying to hold off the bills.
All of that stuff was so unimportant to me. I could not even think. When Gene died, the Social Security stopped. I'm too young to be a widow. I guess a husband is not supposed to die until his wife is 62.

I'm so tired of thinking, so tired of worry. I know what people in concentration camps must have felt like, no hope. Each day is nothing but worry. My mind is mush. There is nothing to look forward to. Will he come out of this and be Gene? He's not Gene now.

Linda Palucci

**It's not him. I am a widow but my husband's body still breathes. I don't know how long I can go on like this. I pace. I am so tired of worry. And the weather is no help. I can't even go outside it is so cold.
Why? Why? We always worked but it was not enough. We don't have a palace. Just a modest home, which we can barely keep. If I could scream, I would.
Today is Wednesday 7:00 AM. Yesterday Cheryl and I took Gene for a ride. We had to go do a couple of errands. All afternoon he tried to badger Cheryl into buying him cigarettes. He drove the poor girl crazy. But no way is he getting them. They may be the one reason he wants to move. Other wise he seems content to sit in his chair.**

He seems to be very tired. He sleeps a lot during the day in bed. I hope this thing we tried works. He's also quiet, except for when he's arguing for a cigarette, then he yells real good. He's not himself at all. Maybe because he's scared. He complains we did not tell him what St. Vincent's, the first hospital, said. But how could we have told him? I'm going crazy myself staying home. Today I am very tired, feel drained like is anything any use? I wonder how it feels to be happy.

It's Thursday AM. Very strange thing. During the night Gene pulled off his socks, then his sweatshirt and sweatpants. Kept saying he was

hot.
Audrey and Louie were here, they said they thought he was better.
Stacy came over later with an ice-box cake Geri made very yummy.

Its Saturday 3:00 PM. Gene went to bed 11:00 PM got up around 12:00 PM and is back in bed again. He sleeps a lot. Hope this is good. Geri, Eddie and Stacy were up. Geri brought him a giant box of candy. Beautiful. He ate a bunch of them. I feel mean not letting him smoke but I know it's best for him.

He's very quiet too. But flares up when I don't know what he wants. Yesterday I had stomach flu, feel a little better today.

But It's so boring hanging around. Scott took Debbie to the hospital last night. She has not been able to eat for a week.

I just received a note from Aunt Ginny. It was very nice. She said her prayers were with us. I cried. It was good to hear from her. I'll have to write her. Today is Monday February 24th. I wrote Aunt Ginny last week. God, the days just drag on. Last week Debbie went back into the hospital.

They sent some IV stuff here for her. Wonder how she is. I hate to call and bother them. Donna is at her Mom's. She's having contractions. Her Doctor wants her off her feet. She's not due for a couple of weeks yet.

Eddie goes for operation the 29th. Tony, goes the 1st of March for cauterization. Lord, what's going on? This dragging around the house all day is awful. It's like time stopped, but the bills go on. We are trying to catch up the mortgage. What a hassle.

I feel alone. I know that sounds dumb but it's like Gene is not really here, just his body. It's not him. I went to church yesterday it felt good. I miss it. Can't wait till spring when I can open house and let air in and go out and clean yard. We've got to clean cellar attic and garage.

Linda Palucci

Chapter 6

Today is February 29th Sat. Leap year. Cat and dog are being pains as usual. Don't know how I got stuck with these two. They chase each other around all day. It's like having two, 2 year olds. Crocuses are leafing, and other plants are poking up. It has really been a winter of no winter.

They put off Eddies operation till Tuesday, because he has a fever. Tony goes in tomorrow, I've got to call Janet.

Gene appears to be doing a little better. Thank God. He says his vision is one instead of two. Yesterday I gave him a couple of cigarettes. I know how much he wanted them. He pleaded so. He is very weak and we have to build up his muscles. He did not sleep as much yesterday as he has been doing.

Audrey and Louie came over for a little bit in the morning. I had just run up for a shower. Cheryl was here. Life is very hectic in one way right now. But boring in another. I'm getting cabin fever, but have no energy to clean.

I just wish I could relax a little, wish I did not have money worries on top of all the other worries. I don't want millions just want to pay bills. It's real windy out there.

This week was Liz Taylor's 60th birthday. She

rented Disney World for the night. They reported the party cost 1 Million dollars.

Some have so much money they don't know what to do with it and others have nothing to eat or a place to live. I wonder how it feels to have no money worries.
Why does anyone need that much money?
I've really got to get Gene to start PT'ing. Karen's wedding is coming soon and so is our grandson. I tell him he needs some strength to hold the baby. Donna could deliver any day.

One night this week, Gene called me into the bedroom. He asked me who was standing by the door. (A man?) I said it was his jacket on the hook. He said 'No' he said it was someone he knew from school, but could not remember his name. He told me to ask him if he wanted a beer. I said we didn't have any. He got mad because I didn't have a beer for 'his friend'.
I think the medicine is making him hallucinate. I think the cat wants my pen. I hear Gene moving around now; it's 10 of 8 AM. Guess I'll get him up and feed him etc.

Linda Palucci

Chapter 7

It's 10:34 Sunday night March 1. We took Gene to the hospital. There was blood in the toilet when he got up, he is in surgery now. Russ, Chris, Cheryl, Peter, Greg, Ann and I are here waiting for hospital to call. We have called everyone and now it's in God's hands, as always. Heather is very restless as if she knows something is up.

He looked so scared, as they wheeled him out. God his eyes just got straight and he was so steady. Bob came up to hospital and Fr. Rocco. We said prayers. I feel it's in Gods hands. Peter just fixed sofa so middle does not sag anymore. Now the wait for hospital to call. It feels as if we have been waiting for 8 months. So it really does not feel any different. This morning at 4:00 AM he called me, I had fallen asleep on the couch. He had wet the bed, first time it happened. Greg helped him upstairs and I gave him a bath. I shaved him as he sat in the tub. Then I put him in our bedroom upstairs where we had set up a single bed. He slept till around 1:00 PM. Later he was in the upstairs bathroom and was constipated. I said, do you want to go downstairs and have some soup? Downstairs, he tried again. When he got up we discovered the toilet was full of blood.

I feel nervous now. Strange feeling. God hope all goes well. These kids watch the stupidest things. They keep switching around. He slept

**in our bedroom last night or this morning.
Around 6:00 AM after his bath. Will I know if?
Now it's 11:15, How long?**

At the emergency room the doctors said he had diverticulitis. It was very serious. He needed an operation immediately, or he had no chance at all. When the doctor explained this to Gene and asked if he would sign for the operation. At first he said "No"
Cheryl exclaimed, "What do you mean No.". I can't remember too clearly all that went on, I was in total shock. Cheryl said you better call Bob or Danny. They were deacons at our church.
I did not have any numbers with me so I called home and asked Greg to call. Shortly after, Bob came.
The doctors planned to perform a colostomy. They told us it would be several hours. We should go home and wait. We did not live far from the hospital.

**Doctor called around 11:45, he's out of surgery, rocky condition. I called Janet, Scott, Russ, Geri, she'll call Audrey.
It's 5:50 AM Monday. March 2, 1992. I slept with Heather. Cheryl going to pick her up, take her to school, then we'll go to hospital. I'm just kind of numb. I just hope the insurance papers got there. God I don't know. I don't want him to suffer. He always told us not to let Dr's keep him alive on machines.**

Linda Palucci

Was it a premonition? So hard, I don't even know my thoughts they keep going around-I'm trying to accept the fact he might die or even worse be half-alive. Heather woke up now she's on sofa. This sounds awful but if he does die I would rather have it happen at hospital than home because the place would be so hard to look at where it happened. I've got to shower and get dressed.

Tony today, Eddie tomorrow, Gene yesterday. All in hospital.
Now Romper Room is on. Cat is being a pest, poor Geri, Eddie and Gene to worry about, Donna could possibly have baby this week. Lord Help us. I too drained emotionally for fancy prayer all I can say is the Lords prayer and help God help.
The doctors were right to send us home last night we would have gone crazy in hospital. We live so close it would be quick to get there. So far I have not heard from hospital. I guess in this case no news is good news.
It's chilly and the sky is gray. Poor Chris has a tooth ache has appointment with Dr. Stein. It's 7:07. Cat and Dog running around like 2 kids. Fr. Rocco was encouraging, Said he has to go in himself around noon, so he'll be at hospital too. He called here 6:55 AM.
He had a colostomy himself last month. Somehow, he had fallen at his house. He had internal injuries. He had fallen when we were at Staten Island.

Linda Palucci

I don't know if it is better for someone to be killed quickly or go though this. God we really need a miracle. Such thoughts in all our minds. I don't even know where to go if he dies, funeral parlor, cemetery.
He can't afford to die, we have too many bills. What if we beat the tumor and his stomach gets him, how ironic. Lord I want all of him back the way he was. This roller coaster of emotions is miserable, one day encouraged next day discouraged. 7:57 I'd better take a shower and get dressed.

Its Thurs. 3/5/92 (Donna's birthday). Yesterday was Ash Wednesday.
Gene's blood pressure way down, his heart rate was way up and it did not look good. We went to Mass and got ashes in chapel at St. Vincent's. It was a scary day. The doctors wanted to go back in and clear out an infection. We were so mixed up. Do we just let him go and avoid more suffering for him or let them operate on the chance he might have beaten the brain tumor and his heart can stand more stress on his body?

It was an agonizing decision. Cheryl called Russ, Scott and Chris to come to the hospital. Bob came, Fr. Rocco was in around 1:00. He did last Rites just in case. We agonized all afternoon over to operate or let it be. All of us were around the bed talking to him. Trying to decide what he would want. We all know he

never wanted to be kept alive on machines and yet if there is a chance for him to come out of this, shouldn't we take that chance?
When I hold his hand it is so hard to just let him go. I love him so much. But I don't want him to suffer any more. Finally around 5:00 I asked him again what he wanted. Something told me to go for the operation. If I didn't and he died would we always wonder if we may have saved him from the divertculitis and his brain tumor may have gone. If God really wants him, He can take him any time. So we told the doctors, yes operate and we came home to wait.

Doctor B, called around 8:30 and said he made it through the operation and was doing as well as can be expected. We called everyone and decided we'd go see him in the morning around 11:00.

I was so shocked last night I could hardly get to sleep. I felt like I was having a heart attack, so I took Maalox, and a muscle relaxer the doctor had given me. Watched the stupid TV until I relaxed enough to sleep.

This morning I got out the yellow pages and looked under funeral homes and cemeteries. I think I have to face facts and look into this. I don't know what to do. I don't want to run up and down to Stamford, Darien and Fairfield for the

Linda Palucci

funeral. Funeral home Stamford? Church Fairfield, cemetery? I need to talk to someone before I need to do it. Do I just pick one out of the Yellow pages? I'm just shaking all over. I almost wish it was over if there is no hope of recovery. I talked to Sue and Ann about finding funeral homes etc. I have to face it, I'll probably need them sooner or later depending on God's time. I feel numb scared they'll call and say he's gone. Every time the phone rings I jump. He's my other half, we were two little 1/2 atoms floating around in space then we found each other and became whole. Now 1/2 of me is going away and I don't feel whole anymore.

Linda Palucci

Chapter 8

Its Fri. 5:00 PM March 6, (Audrey's birthday, also my grandmothers) Today Cheryl and I asked Bob to help us regarding funeral home etc. He did, he knows the area. Now that is settled it's a relief.

Now it's Sun AM 7:00- Yesterday Geri, Audrey, Karen, Stacy, Angie, Ruth, Janet, Tony, Greg, Cheryl and I had a meeting with the Doctor. The Dr. explained Gene is in serious condition, everyone asked questions and we still do not know for sure if he is going to make it. The machines etc. he is hooked to all helping him breathe-but if something happens, they will not keep him alive. We gave orders that if his heart stopped not to try to start it. I can't give the order to remove his breathing machine, I just can't. If God wants him, he can take him, but I can't send him. The vitals look better, his temp was down later.
God I just don't know?? I'm still waiting on the Lord.
Cheryl and I were so tired last night, we stayed home. I called the hospital. The Nurse said he was sleeping and about the same. So I watched Star Trek and tried to relax. Julie and Tim dropped in with a couple of lasagnas.

Gene's color is better and he's less puffy. Today's Friday 13th of March. Donna had Mark 10th 5:15 PM he weighted 7:11. She was home

Linda Palucci

Thurs. 12th. Cheryl and I went to visit her in hospital, St. Joseph's. Gene's pulse came down they changed medicines.
Yesterday afternoon they moved him to the 10th floor, from ICU, room 48. But he's still on breathing machine. I don't know what to do if I can do anything. He doesn't seem to respond to us really. We talk to him but I don't know if he hears us. I'm so mixed up. On one hand I pray for a miracle and on the other I pray the Lord to be merciful and take him. We can't go on this way.
March 17th, Donna and Russ brought Mark up to Gene's room. I got there and saw Gene just looking at him. He had tears in his eyes. Our first grandson. Now we have three grandchildren and one on the way Gene used to say, as ours got older, now we wait for the grandchildren.
Debbie is in and out of hospital. She can't eat, poor Scott is a nervous wreak. As are we all. Now, Maria, Peter's Mom, has a gall stone. I don't know. Hurry Jesus please help. My prayer is still please heal him or take him.

Chapter 9

Mon. March 23, Gene left this world, Sat. March 21, 10:00 AM, **peacefully according to the Doctor. Audrey and I got there just after.**
He **looked tired but finally at peace. I was glad I** made **arrangements two weeks ago because I could not have managed it after. At least when the Doctor asked me who to call, I had an answer.**
Thank God he is out of pain. He hated those tubes. He **has not been able to talk for the past 3 weeks.**
Last night when I left him, I said something which was very difficult. I told him I loved him, always did, always will. I said, 'If you want to go on, I understand. I'll see you later.'

Greg was up to see him, after me. He told me he had also 'given permission to go'. Greg was the last one **to speak to him. Our youngest child. There's a void in our lives.**
This morning the funeral director stopped in for clothes for Gene. That was very hard giving him clothes. They were so familiar. I could just see him getting dressed. We made sure his socks matched, Gold Toe.
I remember how he would take two black socks, hold them under a 100W light, over to the sun-light in the window, be sure they matched, then
he would put them on and put on his boots. I don't know what I am going to do now. I feel

Linda Palucci

like half of me is gone.
I don't even know who I am anymore. I've been Gene's wife for 32 years and now I'm not. So many things to worry about.
I asked Sandy to please do my hair, it's such a mess. Funny thing to worry about, but I know there will be a lot of people who knew Gene. I want to look good for him. It's hard to believe he's really gone.
Cheryl bought me a black dress. I never worn it again and later threw it out.
Cheryl told Heather Pop-Pop went to Heaven because he was so sick. She seems OK, but you never know what's down inside a four year old.
It's now Monday March 30th. The wake was last Tues. It was packed. If a funeral can be beautiful Gene's was. The firemen carried him. Also Gabe, Chris's friend. He wanted to. He and Gene used to talk a lot. The women of the church provided refreshments, God bless them.

Karen's bridal shower was yesterday. Geri's daughter. Cheryl and I went shopping Sat. for a few things and over to Russ's.
I did pretty good at the shower only broke down once, when Audrey smiled and looked like Gene.

God the wedding is going to be hard without

Linda Palucci

him there. My only solace is he's with our Lord. He has no more pain or fear.
A couple of days after the funeral I was unloading the dishwasher. I was feeling very depressed. I was praying. "Lord if I just know he is with you I can handle it."
The phone rang. It was my next door neighbor, Lorette, we
seldom call each other, usually we yell over the fence. She said "Linda, I just had to call and tell you. Last night while I was praying I had a vision of Gene. He was hugging his Mother and saying, "It's so good to be here."

She described him as he looked when he was around thirty. She said he was bending over to hug his Mother. His Mom was only 4' 11".
It was as if my prayer was answered on the spot.
But sometimes I am just overwhelmed and can only handle the very present moment by moment. If I try to think back to before he got sick its worse. It's not we anymore, it's me.

**When people tell a widow, 'Remember the good times.' I can't, that hurts too much.
I put all his clothes in the attic and the boys took a few things.
What do I do with my rings? They don't represent what they used to? I still feel married and then I think but I'm not. How long Lord does this go on? I try to remember other people have had grief too, and they make it.
I thank God for taking him, he was suffering**

Linda Palucci

so.
We have all these thank you notes to write,
they depress us. We do a few
at a time, then we put them away because we
can't handle any more. Why doesn't everyone
put their address on the Mass cards?
Especially people we don't always see. The
wedding and funeral, friends and family.
I feel odd when I look at my rings, but I can't
take them off.
So many people I have not heard from in years
either called, or sent cards. It's sad we don't
see each other more.
My cousin Laurel just called from Virginia. She
invited me down. God, I just feel like jumping
on a train and going for a few days.

Linda Palucci

Chapter 10

It's Saturday, two weeks since Gene went to our Lord. I still get anxiety attacks, have peculiar pains here and there. Sometimes I feel overwhelmed and wander around dazed. Rose Bush called last night. Bob has been gone 7 1/2 years already. Does not seem possible. She says it does get better day by day. I keep thinking of all the people I know who lost people they loved. They survived, with God's help, I will too. I asked her about the rings. She said, after about 6 months she put them on her right hand. Then she put the wedding ring away and just wears the diamond.
I just took mine off for the first time, strange feeling. I put
them in a glass in the china closet. My fingers are kind of puffy anyway. Mine do not fit on my right hand.
Today is Sun, Apr 12. I have been reading books about grief. A good one is Joyce Brothers, 'Widowhood'. God, I hate that word.
I cry at night, out of everyone's sight. I'm trying so hard not
to fold up. The kids don't need more problems. I really would like
to crawl into a corner and pull a blanket over my head. Janet came Tuesday and stayed until Friday. It was good to have her here. Sat Donna and I took Heather, Shannon and Mark to a 'Bunny Fair'.
Matt and Sue are here from Illinois. Today after church a bunch of us went for lunch. Now I am

Linda Palucci

watching 'The Ten Commandments'. I'm very nervous tonight, gas pains. These anxiety attacks are horrible. Sometimes I feel so lost. Mostly at night around 5:00, the time when he usually came home from work. Sometimes I can almost imagine him walking up onto the porch and in the front door. I'm so tight. I feel like my shoulders could touch my ears.
I have absolutely no energy to clean or do anything around the house. Tomorrow I want to get some business done. I'm thinking about going back with Sue and Matt for a few days. Maybe it would be good to get away. There are minutes at a time when I don't think. I can't even say his name to people. I can't go to the cemetery yet.

He's not there, he's with our Lord. I have to see about a stone.
It's still unbelievable this has happened. I really need to find something to do but I need a rest first. I really don't feel like taking on a full time job yet. I want to relax, clean house, have tag sale and travel a little. I have to calm my nerves first.
Today is Tuesday, April 14. Matt and Sue were here last night. I have been bawling for the last hour. This morning I had muffler fixed it was very loud. Gene always took care of those things. I cried at Midas. Then Cheryl and I got emissions sticker and went to look at tomb stones. God, a year ago if anyone told me I would be shopping for tomb stones---. It's like the shock has worn off, I realize Gene is gone, it's unbelievable and I feel as

if I am being torn apart.

I can't even think straight, neither can Cheryl. She wants to move back in, I would like that I think we need each other. It's so hurting. I need time, I guess to find myself. It was good talking to Matt and Sue last night. Finally I could talk about Gene. With everyone else I could not even say his name. I don't know why.
To myself I talk to him, but with other people I can't. It's like too personal. Gene Gene Gene. We had such love. He painted the windows pink for me. I love him so, I need him so how can I go on without him? How do I cope? I feel so alone, even though I am not alone but I feel like only half of me is here. Usually everyone says I am doing so good. If they saw me today they would not say that.
It's almost 3 weeks, tomorrow is 3 weeks. Seems like forever and yet it seems like yesterday. Time is different. It all kind of runs together.

How do people cope without faith? That has been my only comfort. It must be devastating if you do not believe we will all be together again. I found those that believe God's promises, are able to adapt better, there is not the same hopelessness as non believers.
Angie gave me a tree, I can watch the tree grow.
Chris looked so tired tonight. I feel so bad for

Linda Palucci

him. I think it's hitting all of us now. Russ called yesterday just to talk. Scott is in and out. Greg was kind of in the dumps today too.
Today is Friday May 8th. I have gone to 2 Bible studies. I joined 'Cope', a widows group at the Catholic Center. Last night was the 3rd meeting, 2nd for me. It's a 6 week course. I believe it is helping to talk to others who have experienced the death of a spouse. Some appear in worse shape than me.
Cheryl has thrown herself into fixing the yard and making gardens.
I have been trying to clean out the house. I found a box in the cellar with cards in it. From years of Gene giving me and me giving him. I found his 25th Anniversary to me-he had written 'another 25?' and on the 26th Anniversary, he had written 'hope this is the last house 1 fix up'.
Also, there were lots of birthday, Valentine etc, I put them all in a bag and threw them out. I cried a lot that day.
Cheryl and I went out Wednesday. She cried at a pile of dirt and dump trucks. Gene drove a dump truck. We cry at them a lot.
I cried when we went to 'Treeland', a garden store, for more plants. Gene and I used to go there. I finally found a pink watering can. I could just hear Gene saying, 'buy the damned thing', so I did. Fr. R. sent me a letter. He wants to talk to me. I have not gone to church for the past two weeks. I am considering talking to

Linda Palucci

him.

I still remember that sermon he gave one morning. It was 8:00 AM Mass. few people there. He was talking about depression.

He said we should not be depressed if a loved one was dying. I felt like running from the church. I only stayed thinking he would somehow clarify his statement, somehow make it all right. But he didn't. I remember thinking; I'll be depressed if I want to.

I feel like telling him to read some books on grief. He does not understand it at all. You do not 'snap out of it'. You claw your way out of a slippery pit, inch by inch. Reaching up to try to preserve your sanity, often slipping back as memories crowd into your mind bringing tears of hopelessness. The tears are so hot.
It is confusion, anger, fear, guilt. Sometimes wanting people around and other times just wanting to be alone to stare into space. There is no feeling of control over anything.

One Widower, whose wife died March 17th, keeps referring to her in the present tense. Some of these people live alone. That must be far worse. They say they hate coming home to an empty house. However, there was talk of the house 'wrapping it's arms around you. I understand the feeling it's something safe and

Linda Palucci

familiar.

I can't tell if it's any better yet or not.
I guess I'm doing OK, I'm doing a lot of reading on grief and widowhood it helps to realize my feelings are normal. I find it better to take one day at a time. Yesterday I sat for awhile and relaxed. I had gone to 6AM-7AM Bible study and breakfast after. I really do have to keep busy, it does help.
Now we have some more stress. Margaret, Peter's sister, saved her son Michael from a fire he set. They were both burned, Maria had her gall bladder removed. Peter had a tic on him. He went to Doctor, could be Lyme disease. He's on an antibiotic. Hopefully he will not have a problem he caught it so quickly. Very scary.
The past few days have been so cold. Cheryl and I are just exhausted, tired, worn out. I don't feel like doing anything even taking a shower or dressing. I just seem to be existing. Maybe if it gets warm we'll feel better, last weekend was hot, but now it is cold and gray, about 40 degrees.

Cheryl says if you get through this life without killing someone, killing yourself, or going crazy, you should make it into Heaven.
Today is Saturday, May 9th. It is really nice out Cheryl cut the front lawn. I kind of helped rake. Last night we got bureau up to Heather's room. God, I hate Saturday's. Every Saturday

around 9:45 I just get crazy. I finally took a shower and changed my clothes. I just feel very depressed today.

I read another book called "Life Lines" by Lynn Caine. In the book there is a paragraph that says:

-"Yes, it is a crummy life, and yes I hate being single too. Do you ever get used to this life without the one you love? Yes, you do. It is unbelievable, Unthinkable. Impossible. But yes you do. Life goes on, and so do we. Do not let yourself succumb. You must fight, assert your right to live. To enjoy, to flourish. Yes, and to love.

I would like to know if this terrible, terrible ache ever goes away. I really wonder if I can take it. I feel like I'm falling apart. And, I can't understand why my life has to be this way. " –

I feel like this also, it just hurts so much.

I just feel like there is no reason for anything I don't care about anything. I just want to be left alone.

God, will I ever be half way happy again? I just feel dazed. Nothing matters and I am so irritable. I don't want to answer the phone or talk to anyone.

I don't feel like having a tag sale. I just feel like putting everything in bags at the curb.

Linda Palucci

Gene died and I'm in Hell. It's not getting better It's getting worse.

I know I am bitter and self centered. I realize I am wallowing in self-pity. But I can't help it. It is unbelievable I feel so lost.

I don't know if I can go to Karen's wedding. I went to the shower but I was still numb. Now I feel and it is horrible.

I feel guilty that I could not talk to Gene about his death. I could not accept it. The last week in the hospital he had that tube in his mouth and could not talk.

I feel so bad. I could not handle his death well at all. Sometimes I feel like selling the house and flying around till I get on a plane that crashes. Of course, I would take out a large insurance policy for each trip. Made out to the kids.

It's Sunday May 10th, 8:30 AM. I feel very tired and drained. Think I'll not even try to go to church. I have been reading Bible. I'm wondering if I should consider all the time we "knew" he was going to die as "grief period" or only from when he died March 21st?????

I'll have to bring that up at the next widows meeting.

Linda Palucci

I keep thinking I really have to pull myself together and stop walking around in a fog. I don't think I've even reached acceptance yet.
I just saw my Serenity prayer. I have to keep that in mind.
God give me the courage (Serenity) to accept that which I can not change.
I can't change the fact that Gene has died. I must accept it or really lose my mind. (what's left of it). Gene is gone, he's with the Lord. I know this. I'm still here with our family. He loved his family more than anything. I've got to help them and myself to deal with the fact that he is gone. God give me the courage to accept this, and the serenity. Serene Faith in God's love.
It's hard after 32 years to think as one instead of 2. I must let go.
God give me the serenity to accept Gene's death and courage to discover what I should do. I can't just wander aimlessly around indefinitely. I just have to relax and get out. I thank God for the wonderful years we had together.

Today is Tuesday, Apr, no May 12-I can't seem to remember what month I'm in. Sandy came over yesterday, I enjoy her company she's very understanding. Yesterday was a pretty good day.

This morning the weather was pretty good. Don't know what I'll do today. Got Bible study tonight. Strange thing happened Sunday, I was in basement doing laundry-I wandered over to a box

Linda Palucci

of Cheryl's stuff. The old big red Bible was there. I picked it out and looked though it. There was a beautiful Mothers Day card from Gene in the book-it was signed 'All my Love Gene'. It was Mothers Day.
Well, it's Sunday May 17th-I have been having a tag sale since Friday. Sold some junk, made a little bit, but also it has kept me busy. Greg's a pain about it because I'm using the garage.
This coming Thursday will be 2 months, but what is time?

Linda Palucci

Chapter 12

Thursday night was my 3rd widow's group meeting. I do think that's helping a lot. All of the material we get is good to read. I see myself, again and again. I guess I'm experiencing classic reactions.
Thursday on my way to meeting I saw a couple in the store. It made me sad. I can't help thinking why can't Gene be here? It's hard to see couples around our age, just doing ordinary things like we used to do.
I try to rationalize, how sick he was and thank God he did not grow even worse. (What a contradiction that is, grow worse, to grow, means upward).
We were watching home movies. It was strange seeing Gene OK. We noticed a change in his appearance. From Heather's 3rd birthday to Christmas. 10/9/90 to 12/25/90. His Mom had died Nov. 5th, 1990 and he looked haggard at Christmas. I had not noticed until I saw it in the movie. The tumor was found June '91 I wonder if it was starting then.
Scott wants to move in too. God I don't know where to put them. The house is bulging now. More stuff.
I've got to get control of myself. I feel so beaten by life. I wish it would warm up. I just seem to float along without direction.

Next week is Mark's Christening and the week after Karen's wedding. That's going to be so

Linda Palucci

hard without Gene. I really don't feel like going, but have to. It is our grandson and niece.
I looked in paper this morning for a church to go to this morning, but gave that up.
Today is Saturday, June 6, 92. We had the last meeting of the Widows group Thursday. I think it really helped. What a lost looking bunch of people. But our leader, a widow of 10 years, said she thought we would 'make it'. Sometimes I wonder. (This was the 6th meeting of the coping group. There are still monthly meetings of Theos to attend.)

It's always there in the sub-conscience even when not in the front.
I went to the Congregational Church last Sunday. It was so different, but refreshing. The choir was beautiful. Some days are really bad, cry all day. But I found I have to get out of the house. Last night I went to Bonnie's, she's stressed out too. We had a few drinks and dinner it was fun.

This morning I went out for a ride, I was so restless. I just kept driving then I decided to drive to Mahwah, NJ to see Janet. Tony was home. He was surprised and said 'I just dropped your buddy at the airport.' She had gone to visit her family in Michigan and Chicago. (When I got home later, Cheryl said Janet had called me but I was sleeping. She had called to tell me she was going) I had not talked to Cheryl that morning, she was still sleeping when I took off.

Linda Palucci

So anyway Tony and I had lunch and talked for awhile. Gene and Tony were close. Geri introduced Tony, to someone at the funeral, as 'my brother's brother'.

I got home around 6:00. I did not want to be driving too late.
Why do I have the feeling I have to get home? There is no reason at all. But I get this feeling to run home. Maybe with time it will pass. Gene's gone and I feel alone.
It's like I can't even let it come to the front of my mind. I still feel like I'm in orbit. Light headed. I'm proud I went out last night and drove to New Jersey today. A couple of times I felt panic feelings but I prayed and fought for control. I'm surprised I did so good.
I really want to see Laurel. I will soon.
The kids really don't understand my feelings, for 32 years I worried about getting home, now I have nothing to get home for. At least I seem to be more relaxed about the house. Who cares if it's a mess?
Last Saturday was Karen's wedding, that was hard. By the time I got with it, it was time to go home. When they played 'Daddy's Little Girl', I went to the Ladies room. Marilyn was there, another widow, She said, 'There's just some songs you can't take.' We both cried.
The night of the wedding I put my rings on, and have worn them since. Now they make me feel closer to him, they feel natural. But if I let myself think of him I just fall to pieces. He was

**so sweet. God, I
miss him.**

Linda Palucci

Chapter 13

It still seems unbelievable. I feel as if I'm dazed.
Today is July 3rd. Three and a half months. I completed the widow's course, and attend monthly meetings. It did help, I guess. Last week I went to Virginia to visit my cousins Natalie and Laurel. They're sisters. They live about 40 miles apart.
My put my rings in my jewelry box, I'm wearing one of my Mother's rings most of the time. Peter and Cheryl drove me down, and picked me up the following week-end. Laurel's sons took Peter fishing at the Shenandoah River. Peter loves fishing. Cheryl went with us to Bingo. Since then she's been a Bingo nut.

It was good to see them. Their Mom, Aunt Mil was up from Florida. She's been widowed twice. She was helpful to talk to. I still get all kinds of weird pains, feelings and dizzy. Cheryl gets them also.

It was good being with Laurel and Natalie again. We were real close until we all got married and they moved out of state. I had not seen them in years. But it helped me find myself. Cheryl said it was like being with 3 Moms, we're so much alike. Natalie and I visited the Skyline Caverns near where she lives. We went to Bingo games nearly everyday. Checked out quaint little shops and played pinochle.

Linda Palucci

Heather is being very strange. She has had a rash that comes and goes. On the trip she had a fever one night. We took her to 'Sesame Place' and she just seemed to mope through it. Whenever we asked her if she wanted to go on a ride, or do something, she answered 'No, Thank you.'

I guess it was hard for her to watch her grandfather die. She talks about him and heaven. Sometimes she says she wants to go there. She seems to talk about self destruction. For instance let the bad man steal her etc. She seems depressed. I wish I knew what to do.

I don't know how to help myself or any of us to cope. Nothing seems to help. He's always on my mind.

It just doesn't seem to get better. Everyone says it does eventually. I went to visit my cousin Suzette yesterday. I have to force myself to go out. I don't want to become afraid to drive. I seem to get anxiety attacks when I drive. So I put my tapes in and pray as I drive. I seem to ache all over.

A feeling I am becoming aware of is: everything in the universe is conspiring against me, and I feel powerless to change the situation.

It's pretty chilly today 57 degrees this morning. We are putting down a new floor in the kitchen. Also, looking at carpet. But I really don't seem to care very much. I just keep thinking about the last year.

Linda Palucci

Helen Hayes said, for 2 years after her husband died, she was as crazy as she could be and still be at large. She had no conception of what she was doing for many, many months after her husband's death.

We seem to need action, when the best thing is to sit tight. Widows are crazy, sad, lonely. Widows sigh a lot.

To help overcome acute anxiety attacks-move the body.

I gained about 30 pounds over the past 18 months. I realize this was self indulgence. I feel as if I have lost my mind. I can't remember anything.

I also read it is natural not to talk about death with the one who is dying.

After the death, verbal repetition will help. We must talk about what happened, only then does it become real to us. Until we can talk about it and face it we will not recover.

Many Widows reported their religious leader was the least helpful. This was very true in my case. Our priest told Cheryl, "It's been three weeks, get on with your life." He was no comfort to me after the death and very little to our family during Gene's sickness. He was more sympathetic when our cat died last year.

I realize widowers also are grief stricken, not to over look them. Men do not think of themselves primarily as husbands and fathers. Women have to progress from wife, to widow and back to women. The word widow comes from the Sanskrit and means empty.

Linda Palucci

Chapter 14

It's Aug I feel like screaming and screaming. Everything I read says don't make any major moves or decisions for at least a year. But I'm so sick of everything. I really want a nice job or something to do. But I'm so afraid. The world is so scary.
Why should I clean house? My children are grown, my husband is dead. Why do I have to bother to keep the house clean. I did that for years. I'm sick of it. I want to do something, but I don't know what. So I do nothing. I've neglected myself. I don't care what I wear or how I look-nothing matters. Gene is dead. I'm 1/2 dead. Before we know it winter will be here again . God I dread it. House closed up.
I can't even pray. I can't concentrate on anything. Even a book or TV.
Well here I am, it's Aug 26. I have a meeting tonight, Widows.
Just dropped a picture on my toe chasing an ant. Got it. I'm watching Hurricane Andrew on TV. Why do I feel better watching other people be miserable? I can't figure it out. Maybe I can relate to their sorrow? or does it kind of make my problems seem less? or do I like to see other people suffering like me?
Poor Homestead Florida got blown away.
 It seems the government was slow in sending help. If it was someplace we never heard of across the world, they would have been there when the rain stopped.
Friday night Russ and Donna came down to swim.

Linda Palucci

Donna brought sauce, cooked dinner and cleaned up.
Saturday they picked me up and we went to the fire house picnic. Gene had been a volunteer there. Now Russ is a member. It was good to see everyone. I felt like I went into a time warp. Everything was the same. A few new kids and new faces, but still the same. I could almost pretend Gene was there with the guys. A few times it seemed like I saw him. God, does this horrible hurt ever go away? No matter how many people are around me, I am still alone.

It's hot today, I vacuumed the pool. Cool job. I feel like I'm nowhere or no-one, just a burden on the wheel of life. I feel like God forgot about me.
Last night on TV there was a guy who killed some people in June of 91. I can't help wondering why is my wonderful Gene dead, and that scum alive.
Surprise, Cheryl discovered she is pregnant. I don't know how we feel about this. Guess we just go with the flow. She is due somewhere around the end of March beginning of April.
Scott and Debbie had a beautiful little baby girl, Amanda. September 23, at 7:04. 18 inches 6.2 pounds. Debbie had an easy delivery. Only 19 mins for the real delivery once she got started. We all are tired but happy. She is beautiful. Scott is thrilled. Thank God everything is fine.

Today is Sunday Nov. 25th. Wednesday was 7

months. Last Monday I took off and drove down to Virginia by myself. I decided within an hour. I just felt like getting into the car and driving. I called Laurel and made sure she would be home, packed a bag and left. It was 4:00 in the afternoon.

Only had 2 small problems. I had forgotten to pack underwear. I bought some the next day. And I really didn't have enough cash for tolls. So in Maryland I had to find a bank that would give me some cash from my bank card. I did. And arrived at Laurel's around midnight.

Even when I got to Virginia I could have kept driving. Laurel lives on a farm. It is so peaceful there. The stars are so bright. I love to look at the sky, it is so big there. No buildings in the way. We went to Bingos and shopping and over to Natalie's. She lives on a mountain. What a view. Cheryl was upset I drove down myself. But I had to prove I could do it. I did fairly well; Natalie and I had gone shopping. Driving though a Mail I saw a red and black dump truck like Gene used to drive. I got all teary.

But Thursday night I felt homesick, I don't know why. Just felt very lost. I didn't feel like I belonged there. But I don't feel like I belong here either. I don't feel like I belong anywhere. I feel so lonely and lost.

I got a few anxiety attacks on the way home

Linda Palucci

Friday. Most of these were from construction work. Dump trucks and men standing around in flannel shirts, like Gene used to wear. I took my time, traffic was heavy, but there was no hurry. Just being by myself and having to make decisions for myself gave me confidence.

Heather gave me such a welcome when I got home. She's such a joy.

Today Donna had a birthday party for Russ. I felt quite depressed being at our son's birthday without Gene. I felt like I don't belong there either. God, I'm getting so fat, got to lose it. Does it ever get better?

Cheryl, Peter, Heather and I went down to Maria's last night. She was going to a dance at the church. I was going to go with her. But when we got there I changed my mind.

1. It cost $30.00. 2. I was tired.   3. I was depressed and felt I would just sit there like a lump. 4. I had nothing decent to wear. Besides Peter was coming down with a cold and I didn't want him to have to hang around waiting for me to drive me home again.

Cheryl just came downstairs, she said she was depressed too. She had gotten into the shower and cried. It just seems so hopeless.

Gene used to talk about insurance and what would happen if he died. I used to tell him if he died nothing would matter. And it's so true.

I still feel like nothing matters. Except the kids if it would not hurt them I would feel

like I didn't care if I lived or died. It's just so hard. The only good thing about insurance would be not to have to worry about money too.

I talked to Doris, the founder of our widows group. I explained how I feel like I don't belong anywhere.

She understood. She said, 'When you are out you want to be home, and when you are home you want to be out.' That's it precisely.

She explained I was Restless and Searching. How true. Searching for someone I love and can't find.

To become me again I must free myself from the incapacitating effects of the hurt. I need the resilience to recover.

I feel so alone. Unconnected. Dishes in the sink. So what? Not important.

Today is Sun Nov 1st. This past week I have been serving on Jury Duty. That's another book. But it was good to have somewhere to go at a certain time. It was fun going to lunch with people. There were some nice men and women, I enjoyed being out.

I think jury duty is helping me think again. Maybe now I could look for a job.

Scott and Debbie got an apartment. They took the living room set, which is theirs. I had thrown mine away when they came. Gene's chair was ruined and the couch was not too stable either.

Cheryl and I bought a new living room set. Now the house is different. I think it's easier to have

it all changed. We appear to be thinking clearer. As **if our brains are waking up.**
I have started to look for work. Of course the economy is bad. Jobs are scare. I really need the money. Everything is behind. Also I need a life.
I went for a few interviews. At one there was a very nice gentleman. I explained my husband had died and I needed a job. He was so understanding. But I got all teary. He said it was OK to cry, I said sure, but not at an interview.

Anyway, I signed up at a temporary agency I worked out of before. They found me an assignment which is long term. So now I am working again. It really is good. If I had been working when Gene died it would have been easier to keep working where I was familiar. But trying to find a new job was hard.

The period from Thanksgiving to the end of the year was difficult. Thank God I was working. Twelve years ago on Thanksgiving Day my Mother died. My Mother-in-law was two years, November 5th.

The Holiday season without Gene was awful. We decided not to buy for the adults, only for the kids. Cheryl put up the tree a couple of weeks before Christmas. Heather enjoyed it. We stressed what the season really is, the Birthday of Jesus.

Linda Palucci

Christmas day, after Heather opened her gifts, we had breakfast. Then Greg went to his girl friend Anna's house for dinner. Cheryl, Peter and Heather went down to Maria's for dinner.

I was going to go, but was so gloomy, I did not even want to sit around making small talk. I could not even pretend to be sociable. So I stayed home and watched TV. Chris was home and I cooked some chicken and that was it.

Two days after Christmas Cheryl took the tree down. Gene always took it down; she just wanted to get it out of sight. He was so much a part of the Christmas tree. He was so careful to wrap everything and put it away just right.

I was glad when the whole thing was over. Then I had to get though January 16th, our anniversary. Somehow I survived the ordeal. Hopefully next year will be a little easier.

So here I am a year after Gene died. I have volunteered to teach reading to adults who are illiterate. Helping others helps you.

Years ago Widows wore black for at least a year. Some forever. Some still do. We should be able to wear a sign, "Fragile, Wounded Widow", "Hurting Human" or some such thing.

I still have sad times. Sometimes A song, seeing something he loved at the grocery store, someplace we used to go together. Widows seem to do a lot of crying while driving. It's hard going some place and knowing you have to go home alone. Doris had advised us to take our own cars when possible. That way if we felt we wanted to leave we could. That was good advice.

It still seems unbelievable.

I realize I'm never going to be the same person I was before he died. I know my whole life has changed.

We have gone to a few more single dances. I have been flattered, pursued a bit, danced with a few nice men. I see people having fun. It reminds me I am still a women, it feels pretty good. I've even started to diet.
It is good to get out where there is life. We all have to accept what has happened. It's not what happens to a person but how we react that matters.

I know a women who has been a widow for 10 years, she's still moaning about it in every conversation. She acts like it just happened yesterday.

I'm not looking for romance. Just want to feel like a person again. I enjoy my new friends. We can relate to each other, all four of us were once ½ of a couple. There is a sadness in each of us. I guess will always be there. We are recovering, we don't want to stay home and cry the rest of our lives.

Linda Palucci

I love him, I miss him, and wish with all my heart he was still with me.

I don't know what the future hold, I rely on Romans: 8:28 " All things work together for the good, for those who love God".

Linda Palucci

Some poems I wrote during this time:

Morning Grief

Just before the dawn,
When it's neither day nor night When it
really isn't dark, Neither is it light.
I stare at the sky, Savoring the silence,
Before the world awakes.
There are no demands upon me, Just me
and God above.
And, I cry to the sky Why did you take my
love?
My life is, as this moment, Climbing from
the dark
I can't quite see the light Beyond my broken
heart.
"They" say I will recover, Whoever, "They"
may be.
Please hurry God, And send the dawn. For
now, no light I see.

***

At first there were
two, then we
became one.
Not really one, But two halves.
Now one is gone, and one is left.
But I only feel like a half.

Linda Palucci

***

Who am I? I cry.
    To the sky
    above. For I
    lost myself,
    when I lost
    my love. I'm
    no longer we
    Now I'm just
    me.
    I'm no longer a half -
    And, I'm not really
    whole. Who am I? I
    cry
    From the depths of my soul.

Linda Palucci

Gregs High School Graduation

Linda Palucci

Heather our1st grandchild (Cheryl & Peter's daughter)
Gene is sitting in his chair.

Linda Palucci

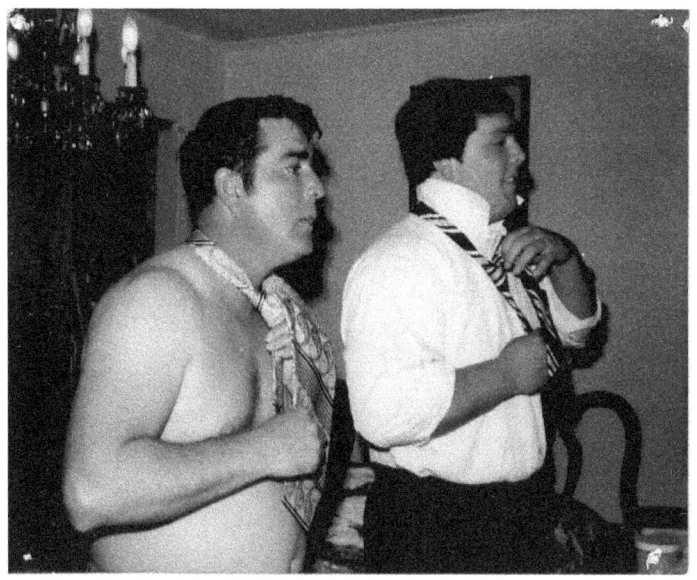

Gene was showing Russ how to tie a tie

Linda Palucci

The family in better days

www.ingramcontent.com/pod-product-compliance
Lightning Source LLC
Chambersburg PA
CBHW031931080426
42734CB00007B/630